W9-BXQ-159

CELEBRATING THE PEOPLES AND · CIVILIZATIONS OF AFRICA™

THE
BENIN KINGDOM
OF WEST AFRICA

John Peffer-Engels

The Rosen Publishing Group's
PowerKids Press™
New York

Published in 1996 by The Rosen Publishing Group, Inc.
29 East 21st Street, New York, NY 10010

First Edition

Book design: Kim Sonsky

Photo credits: Cover, pp. 4, 7, 8, 11, 12, 15, 16, 20 © Phyllis Galembo; p. 19 © Eliot Elisofon/Eliot Elisofon Photographic Archives, National Museum of African Art, Smithsonian Institution.

Peffer-Engels, John, 1966
    The Benin Kingdom of West Africa / by John Peffer.
        p.   cm. — (Celebrating the peoples and civilizations of Africa)
    Includes index.
    Summary: Describes the history and customs of the Edo of Benin who live in the rain forest of Nigeria and are known for their ivory and brass art.
    ISBN 0-8239-2334-7
    1. Bini (African people)—History—Juvenile literature. 2. Bini (African people)—Social life and customs—Juvenile literature. [1. Bini (African people)] I. Title. II. Series.
    DT515.45.B56P44 1996
    966.9′3—dc20   96-7580
                                                                                        CIP
                                                                                         AC

CONTENTS

WHO ARE THE EDO OF BENIN?

The Kingdom of **Benin** (beh-NEEN) is 1,000 years old. Benin is famous for its ivory and brass art. The people of Benin are called **Edo** (EE-doh). They live near the **Niger** (NY-jer) River in the rain forest of **Nigeria** (ny-JEER-ee-ah), a country in West Africa.

Long ago, many Edo were brought as slaves to North and South America. They took their religion and art with them. But many Edo stayed in Africa too. Today, the Edo go to school and work like the people you know. Some live in cities in Africa and Europe.

◀ The Edo of the Benin Kingdom have a long and proud history.

5

TRADE AND MARKETS

Long ago the Edo traded ivory, fine cloth, and pepper with Europeans. Now they sell rubber made from tree sap.

Each week the Edo hold outdoor markets. People from different villages come to meet and share news. Soap, dishes, medicine, fruit, cloth, and kola nuts are all for sale at the market. People chew bitter-tasting kola nuts when they work in the hot sun. Kola is now used to make soft drinks called colas.

Many stores in Benin offer the same services as stores in big cities. ▶

VILLAGES

Edo forest villages are connected by rivers and roads. Edo grandparents, parents, and children usually live in the same house. Men live in the front of the house. Women and children sleep and cook food in the back. At night, the family sits on straw mats. They share tales of magic animals and tell stories about the ancient kings of Benin.

◀ Everyone gathers around to watch two boys play a board game in Benin City, the largest city in Benin.

MANNERS AND MEALS

Good manners are important to the Edo. When the Edo meet each other they say, "**Koyo**," (KOH-yoh), which means "Be lucky." After a delicious meal, guests say, "**Kada**," (KAH-dah), "May you always be rich."

The Edo grow yams and other vegetables in their gardens. The whole family works together in the garden. Edo women cook with a tasty red oil made from palm fruit. Young men climb trees in the forest to gather the oily palm fruit. Men also hunt wild animals and fish in the rivers for food.

Some Edo buy vegetables, such as okra, at the outdoor market. ▶

GODS

The Edo believe the world was created by **Osanobua** (OH-shan-oh-bwah). Osanobua made other gods too. **Olokun** (OH-low-koon) is the god of the sea. He brings wealth and happiness to those who pray to him. His favorite color is white. The Edo believe that the color white is clean and cool. People who pray to Olokun paint their bodies with white clay from the river. They draw pictures on the ground with white chalk and dance on top of them. Olokun blesses them and dances with them. Olokun takes away anger and makes a person "cool."

◄ Like all who pray to Olokun, these boys are painted with white clay before a special ceremony.

13

FAMILY ALTARS

Every house has a special **altar** (ALL-ter) to **honor** (ON-er) relatives who have died. The Edo believe that respecting their old people and their gods helps them live in peace, wealth, and happiness.

Families also have altars to honor the head and the hand. For the Edo, wisdom and good luck come from the head. Success in life comes from the hand.

Each family has an altar or shrine to honor their ancestors. ▶

BENIN CITY AND THE OBA

Benin City is the capital of the Kingdom of Benin. Thousands of people live in Benin City. Most of these people are Edo. The Edo king is called the **Oba** (OH-buh). His palace is in Benin City. He prays for the happiness of the Edo people. Many chiefs help rule the kingdom. They say the Oba never eats or sleeps, and his feet never touch the ground.

◀ The Edo believe that the Oba is very powerful.

ART AND THE OBA

At festivals, the Oba displays his wealth and power. He wears a crown and suit made of red coral beads.

The Oba's palace is filled with beautiful art made of ivory, brass, and wood. Special artists make sculptures for the Oba. Long ago, Benin artists made pictures out of brass that recorded important events in Benin history. About 100 years ago British soldiers took many of these pictures and sold them. Benin art can now be seen in museums in the United States and Europe.

The Edo are known around the world for their beautiful sculptures of brass and wood. ▶

THE QUEEN MOTHER

The Oba's mother has a place of honor among the Edo people. She has her own palace. Artists make sculptures especially for her. She helps her son and the chiefs rule the kingdom. The Queen Mother and Edo princesses decorate their hair with beautiful red coral beads. Red is a symbol of royalty in Benin. Coral is valuable. It comes from deep in the sea.

◀ The Queen Mother and Edo princesses often wear beautiful jewelry made from red coral beads.

ANIMALS

Some animals are strong **symbols** (SIM-bulz) in Benin. The Edo believe that pythons are messengers from Olokun. Pythons bring good luck to the people and the land. Python snakes are colored like beautiful rainbows. The Edo believe that the Oba can change into any animal, even an elephant or a leopard. Elephants are powerful like the Oba. Their tusks are made of valuable ivory.

GLOSSARY

altar (ALL-ter) Table used to make offerings to a god.

Benin (beh-NEEN) Kingdom in West Africa.

Edo (EE-doh) The people of the Benin Kingdom.

honor (ON-er) To think highly of.

kada (KAH-dah) Edo for "May you always be rich."

koyo (KOH-yoh) Edo for "Be lucky."

Niger (NY-jer) River in West Africa.

Nigeria (ny-JEER-ee-ah) Country in West Africa.

Oba (OH-buh) The king of the Edo.

Olokun (OH-low-koon) Edo god of the sea, of coolness, and of wealth.

Osanobua (OH-shan-oh-bwah) Edo god who created the world.

symbol (SIM-bul) Thing that represents something else.

23

INDEX